T0161532

Sia, Beau
First edition

ISBN: 978-1-945649-39-4

Edited by Saul Williams
Proofread by Rhiannon McGavin
Cover design by Shaun Roberts
Cover art by Beau Sia
Editorial design by Julianna Sy

Not a Cult
Los Angeles, CA

WELL PLAYED

PRAISE FOR WELL PLAYED

Steve Nguyen, Author of *To Baby, From Daddy*

Well Played is a profound reckoning with extensive social, political and philosophical commentary from one of America's greatest spoken word artists. Sia's amazing catalog of poetry shows us that we have so much to learn about ourselves and the rapidly evolving world we live in.

Norman Lear

Check out Beau Sia's work, (He's your neighborhood poet), if you want to A) Be inspired, and B) Feel the warmth and comfort in the embrace of his every phrase.

Amber Tamblyn, Author of *Era of Ignition: Coming of Age in a Time of Rage and Revolution*

Well Played is the receipt of a revolutionary awakening, a damning and vital excavation of whiteness, masculinity and identity, written by one of America's most potent and important living writers.

Shane Koyzcan, Author

Honesty is the rarest form of bravery; it can look like self-immolation if all you focus on is the pain. With *Well Played*, Beau Sia asks us to look at the light honesty can cast. This is a book I will read many more times. This is the kind of writing I want to aspire to.

Margaret Cho, Comedian

Scintillating and sensual words, a dynamic and daring work from an important artist. I'm extremely excited about knowing Beau and reading Beau and can't wait for you to read and know him too.

Bob Holman, Poet/Founder of The Bowery Poetry Club

Well Played is a raw anger word dance, not to be read sitting down. The world has never seen a book like this one, nor needed it more. Wisdom language rocks activation and Beau Sia is the fuse.

The Late Denizen Kane, Poet

Lost-found manchild in the unpromised land, Chinoy MC, Rock Steady ambassador, OK player, bicoastal refugee, slam phenom, Hollywood interloper. Beau has been transmogrified 1000 times over. But through it all, he is and remains the bardic voice of a generation, bottling the lament of immigrant America's golden soul, setting the jar on the windowsill to cool and light our way. Read and see it is so.

George Watsky, Artist

Well Played is the fiercest work yet from Beau Sia. It is a necessary confrontation, a roadmap to growth that refuses to erase the potholes. It left me shaken loose, taking personal inventory, and challenged, as I have so often felt in admiration of Beau- to do better.

Bao Phi, Poet, Author of *Thousand Star Hotel*

Here is a courageous book by a veteran of the performance poetry game not satisfied with resting on his laurels. Growth, as an artist and a person, is as painful as it is necessary. Beau Sia has generously given us a window into that journey, where his sharp lens burns as intensely on himself as it does on the world we all live in. He asks, "what can you see in me/when no longer/trying to place/where I belong/in the city of checked boxes?" To read this book is to instigate necessary questions, of the poet and of the one reading the work.

Jenny Yang, Writer/Comedian/Actor

Beau is one of the few writers whose words can both agitate and comfort the soul. He is a singular voice who has inspired so many of us to be fearless in standing in the power of our own.

Adriel Luis, Artist & Curator

Well Played is a survival guide that understands that the point isn't just to survive, but to flourish. Beau's writing has always inspired me to become a better poet, but these poems inspire me to be a better human.

INDEX

FOUND IN OTHER DIMENSIONS

THE ONLY ASIAN AT THE PARTY

Tends to dress *unrealistic*.

Arrives before
things really get started.

Laughs while
watching the corners
of everyone's eyes.

Holds his drink
like they do in Bond movies.

Has one too many,
    but not *toooo* many.

Knows the exits,
              bathrooms,
        & what the
          signature cocktail is.

Has creatively explained
where he's from 3 times already.

Felt a white woman
linger on his shoulder
              toooo long.

He looks good enough to eat.
A burst of flavor eager to be washed down.

    He wants to know where
    everyone is eating afterwards,
    but knows
    you don't ask that here.

Reminds someone of
Dave who was *soooo* crazy in college.

Later gets mistaken for
a valet.

Later overhears some shit
about China
he walks away from.

Later puts a memory
in his pocket
            like he accomplished something
            just by being invited.

Isn't captivating enough
to be in the movie version.

Has a white girlfriend
that would've made this night
less defensive.
                And more awkward.

The only Asian at the bash
is a bigger deal
        to the Asians
        looking in from the street.

He treats their envy in the afterwards
        as treasure
        after leaving feeling empty.

Isn't remembered by those he met,
but everyone keeps saying,

"What a colorful event!"

HASBEEN

holy shit it feels good
to be a hasbeen.

'cuz you know me.

hasbeen an addict to
writing until
I'd forgotten my face.

rage until
I lost my voice.

regret until
I started slow deathing the future.

I hasbeen a son
blaming his parents
for america.

a friend
getting got 'cuz
never taught boundaries
with white people.

a partner
chasing love
to run from everything
I don't like about myself.

I hasbeen forcing the issue
instead of listening to my heart.

I hasbeen unaware of anxiety
until I coma'd at the party.

I hasbeen insecure
to the point of
staying on my knees for belonging.

hasbeen the poet
who helped white poets feel diverse.

hasbeen the poet
who gave passes to white men's verse.

hasbeen the poet
hiding worthless
at the expense of others
through brat expressions
of power.

hasbeen the poet
who almost kept working with def.

hasbeen the poet
who almost got stuck in the beat's bedroom.

hasbeen the poet
who almost didn't see the plot twist
in the legend's story.

I accept whatever fate
befalls me.

'cuz i hasbeen
too hung up on getting mine.
too victimhood as denial tool.
too fuckboy in a love ploy.

who hasbeen
so depressed shutting it out.

so depressed letting it be definitive.
so depressed
wondering why my life
didn't turn out the way

early accolades
suggested it would,
based on all the things
I read by colorless
poets in the quiet room.

didn't see that the trophies,
the trinkets,
and the treats of triumph
weren't the only things
I, hasbeen.

stuck in diminishing returns
of celebrated angst,

was once the dragon sleepwalking
through caverns claiming golden.

waking in truth
to release this regret,
beginning to let go
of all that deludes
in the standing O.

standing in my own,
growing out of
all the things I've been
that would never
fulfill this destiny.

TAKE A STEP TO NOT DISHONOR TIME

keep working on not living
in regret.

keep writing to nurture
working on this resentment.

got myself in mantra mode
                                eternal
    on my
    everything happens for a reason shit.

been digging through the crates
                                for them clues.

transform bad hands into
all-in double ups.

remember, I'm the type of dude that
                could treat a single failure
                as evidence
                my whole being all for naught.

feeding myself compassion patience posts
to take the edge off this judgery.

can't see it as a waste
I long to re-do as a boon,
        'cuz 1995 will never return,
        no matter
                        how much sci-fi I worship.

instead, I return
to the archetypes of my greatest lessons
                        (which is something
                        I can prepare for).

so I cut my bootstraps off
to not do it the colonizer's way.

& I keep waking up
not killing myself,
                    so I push on towards
                    not blaming myself
                    or the world
                    for where these choices led.

hold back on labeling myself
cautionary tale absolute,
                    (still breathing, after all).

excavating mistakes
to mine brighter futures
                    (but don't rush ahead).

when will I get there
gives way to
just keep swimming.

using what adds,
even if it's corny.

even if right now
I'm still hung up
          on how I
          should've walked away
                              from you
when nadine told me
who you are.

everyone I played
dungeons & dragons with.

the trope
who ran the comic book shop.

whichever priest we happened upon
at st. james.

the cartoons I watched after school.

all the outcasts
as the closest I'd get to seeing myself on screen.

every other kid
getting duped by john casablancas.

how I remember the swim team.
how I remember band camp.
how I remember honors whatever.

magazines I rifled through
for secret codes.

who the books on influence
were all by.

all my teachers, even
in ancient japanese literature.

the face of everyone I had a crush on.

the face of
everyone who has ever rejected me.

been reminded at every intersection
who america is for.

    listening to color commentary.
    studying oscar speeches.
    watching the olympics
    and praying
    I don't have to answer for china
    on monday.

the supervisor
beating glass ceiling into my father.

co-workers seeing spycraft
in everything
my mother does differently.

who we lived out
romance novels with
in the suburbs.

growing up,
never had to dream of
a white christmas.

it was a given
year round.

NOT *ALL* WHITE MALE *POETS*

lament out loud about black poets
getting all the gigs.

are sick & tired of hearing another
poem *attacking* them at the slam.

want you to introduce them
to your asian friend for fetish finally.

keep a non-white on standby to
diversify the alabaster hall.

never uplift others
to within striking distance
of threatening their power.

think their poem about mailboxes
way deeper than it is.

are upset they don't have a cave canem,
oblivious to how everything before
was their cave canem.

have no concept
of everything
they don't have to think about
in order to be called poet.

have never lived
the quick trigger firing of being labeled difficult.

think that every after party is great
as long as the alcohol is free.

will never understand the yuck
of being an exotic toy

for a drunk poet's
future work.

doesn't get
        their entitlement to touch
    and the harm
    of ignored boundaries.

can't connect any of their success
to the undergrad roommate
who now runs silicon something.

can act a royal fool and not
have it condemn their demo.

only need the proof of concept
of seeming confident.

haven't cut the cord to supremacy
or noticed it sticking out their shirt.

claim bootstraps for everything
that was access denied others.

prefer stealing ideas from women,
because what consequence if called out?

get treated like the first for writing it
7 years later.

have been embraced
    by one of the most talented asians in the world
    who's lived this game.

are in circles
        where their allyship
        dissipates among red flags.

are writing a book to proclaim
all the things they possess mastery over.

are trying to figure out how to flip this script
and mark themselves victimized here.

have a perfectly reasonable reason
for these musings
that wouldn't hold up in a court of law.

have too much time on their hands
wasted on orchestrating dismissal,

instead of making the man in the mirror
more than a karaoke song
they think will get them laid.

ODE TO THE UNSAID BEFORE OUR SEPARATE WAYS

it's not your fault
I'm prone to enabling racism.

that I retreat inward
with each dismissal of what's foreign
to your upbringing.

how I rationalize where we don't go
when excessing on sunday.

in the shadows I keep sifting
through how I've kept it comfortable
to belong.

don't know if I got such notions overhearing
suspicions of immigrant maids.

or mild takes on all women
        so long as white women are first.

what conditioned me to believe
your approval worthy
        of contorting myself
        into the easiest shape
        to digest with bespoke olives?

was I really your friend
        if I kept choosing a dishonesty
        shown as what
        would cause you to embrace me?

forgive me for expecting you
to listen to what would require
challenging your ancestors.

thought my example would inspire
seeing me alone in an all white house.

wanted so badly to be a symbol
of what you haven't worked on,

instead of an excuse that all of the work
already done
    by putting me in your hand computer.

sitting in the sandbox,
    sorting through signs I ignored
    that are haunting future choices.

    the motive of the candlestick
    cloaked in the presentation of praise.

    zen master label just
    bald chink stereotype missing the mark.

    this depression
        more a gateway to your hurt
        than compassion towards my pain.

wondering in looking back
    why I never said what would've freed us
    before the go fuck yourself.

why I returned to the cotton
that never nourished.

why I silenced myself further into spaces
that had no room for more than proclamation.

why I danced fabulously to deflect the harm of
the willful ignorance sing-a-long.

how expectation to see us absolute
within your trophy case

is the proof
that leads me out of
the prison of your memory.

REVENGE KEEPS TRYING TO FAIL YOU,

it woulda been legendary,
but that don't make the cake rise.

learned the hard way that
          just 'cuz I'm good at it,
          don't mean I should.

though it's such a comforting bottle
                    to drink from.

such a convenient container
        for what's unresolved between people.

feels like the best option
          isolated in feelings
                        lost in space time.

but really tho,
would they see the pain they caused
in my destruction of their lives?

would they learn how to bring
less harm into the world
if their reality became filled with harm?

would they wonder how to
get right with me
if I became the reason
for all the wrong
        of their falling apart
        at the seams?

sure, I'd never be forgotten.
but what ego is this
                    that makes mockery
                    of pain
        by using it
        to justify irrevocable hurt?

to plan a demise
        always brings more death with it.

there is no growth
in gorging on illusory fruits.

if I'm to evolve out of wasting rage
on getting theirs,

must resist the obvious seduction
     and lean into
         the difficult understanding.

this revenge
I obsessed early eras with
will poison the river   if I let it.

those who have left me breaking
are not responsible
for what was broken before we met.

those I once dreamed revenge for
are merely struggling to piece together
the price of their hurts unchecked.

may I never follow them into
     the tunnel of blindness
     as I work the truth

that vengeance
was never mine.

AS A CHILD I DREAMED OF WAR AS

the clarity of the kill shot.
               defeat
             in the slaughtered's surrender.

victory, a flag.
       behold the undeniable truth!

    flipping through tanks of
    forgotten eras.

    reading how the longbow
    became the standard.

    confined myself to the library
    and countless books
    on vanquished enemies.

saw the shaping of the world
through the eyes of destruction.

        saw the history
        of winning
        tied to the death of millions.

    saw the righteous words justifying,
    and let them wash over
    my junior high days of rejection.

failing in the hallways
to convince her I'm valentine-worthy,

        went through magazines
        filled with magazines
        that numbered absolute power.

unable to convey
the geometry of otherness
in the seating arrangement,
        studied legends rising
        from a rubble of blood
        that did not listen.

raised in a town that
saw me as the face of
wrong in this country,

        retreated into stories
        of enemies
        that learn lessons
        the worst way.

        mistook the battles of my life
        as destruction's cycles.

'cuz diplomacy never caught the eye
        like a heat-seeking missile.

'cuz relationships
never the focus
        during the chapter
        regaling the siege.

'cuz no one looked over my shoulder
to say, *that's supremacy with a ribbon.*

        that's extinction with champagne.

        that isn't power,
        it's weakness willing to kill
        all that challenges it.

not that I would've noticed
behind the re-enforced drawbridge
of my pent-up.

as if I hadn't made false idol
of the war machine
to quell my raging lack.

oh, how I mourn
the child who never gets to reach back
            into the chest of memory.

unable to
find the worn toy
    misplaced beneath the staircase
                    of the palace.

        spending their grown
        pretending explosions
        aren't still ringing
        in their ears.

prayer for us who
were taught death
        as a failed method
        of protection.

may we sell the passages
back to the distributor.

may the desire to
taste another's defeat
        not become
        the hill we die on.

THEY KNOW NOT WHAT THEY DO

harvard doesn't make them
as educated as they'd like to believe.

connections are not
the value of character.

the resume is subjective
                everywhere.

those unaware of this
        stuck in the molasses of bias.

    such conviction
    to distract from one's oblivious.

the careless word
that turns a question
            into blame's champion.

the careless act that harms a whole
                to serve a sum.

the careless direction
    that misses the vulnerable
    to appease
                those who squeak
                vulnerability's brand loudest.

teaching the book of good
            leads us down the path of death.

    we cling to learning
    built from the failings of conquest.

        in the unconscious quest to confirm,
        miss all that's rigged
        in favor of self-deception.

for they know not
what they refuse to see.

for they know not who
they are.

more interested in the badge
than the skill.

obsessed with the headline
over the story.

wreaking havoc
in the inherited permission
to commit false choices.

be careful
with whom you consult,
for they may not know
what they advise.

only how they want you
to treat it.

YOUNG(ER) ASIANS SAVING UNCLE BEAU
FROM DEFEATEDERY

saw you on the tubes
    beloved by the numbers.

    instead of the joke,
        you are the reason for the love.

the way you sashay unashamed
        across borders
        in every gesture
   got me
   all choked up.

obama vibes
witnessing possibility
    many unsure
    we'd see in our lifetime.

many, who never
   had a portal
   to rise less alone
   in nebraska.

many, who fought
   generations
   for dignity doled out
   in scraps.

many, who lost themselves
   accumulating achievement
   in contexts
   that only held space
   for the marketing of equality.

what we thought we were doing
clearly now

        the setting of conditions
        for what you are doing.

you got us so done with
        feeling compelled to explain
        to racism's satisfaction.

you pushed the room to
welcome the wondrous nuance of story.

you expanded the range
that led to
                diaspora beyond the east of us,
                culture beyond the food of us,
                lifestyle beyond the lens of them.

no fucks to give their stereotypes,
expressing thineselves 'til they can't compute.

hyping my hope
that each of us able to
tie-dye our wardrobe
however the fuck we want.

your courage
revives the fire I put out
on my way to the tonys.

watch your content
to remind me what I gave up
chasing chalk caresses.

grateful that
when I dropped the torch
nodding out in a fog,
you picked it up
without waiting for a blessing,

& I'm proud of what you've done
towards transforming this age.

DINOSAUR EXHIBIT

I took money from the smithsonian,
via the koch brothers,
because I couldn't pay the rent.

     the vulnerable
     are not supported enough
     to make healthier choices.

wrote their night
so board members would be comfortable
saying what I'd scripted.

     ain't enough pathways
     out of poverty's concessions.

guided by
what committee notes inferred,
made sure distinguished guests
never heard connections
between fossils and oil.

     as a child, I consumed fantasy
     to protect myself from reality.

erased myself in a suit to not
stand out while backstage.

erased myself in english to let
soundcheck be what
scientists said would work.

erased myself in the great hall,
so none would wonder
how ineffective their donations
to those scraping for change.

in my fear of eviction, I swallowed
the pill that provided the bond.

kompromat
begins way before
you meet the
evil mastermind.

racism is a subtle knife
cutting into other dimensions.

power is always eager
to show its grace
        disguising the price
        of its will
        on the world.

I was paid handsomely
for typing out
the soft opening of a space
built as testament
to the role we have
when
the wealthy want
to empty the source.

THOSE WHO POWER ON YOU

do not do them how they do you,
though they'll attempt the imprint.

trauma can seal the future
if presented as a given.

if you cannot be a hammer,
does that make you a nail?

if you become the hammer,
who do you strike down first?

if the hammer
only shows you its force,
will you ever learn
how to extract what's false?

never let only being taught the stick
prevent you from living the carrot.

regurgitating
what kept you down
    only reflects
    what those
    who've held power
    tell you is powerful.

    how they prop up the obsolete
    as universal law,

            when we've clearly
            grown out of dial-up.

but what happens
when we freaky friday
into roles we've only witnessed
beneath the heel of?

will we find darker people
to justify pressing down
to stay standing?

will we erase what challenges
our harmful?

will we wreck lives for
pittling nuisance?

will we burn the evidence
to keep our elevation?

will we ever grow out
of the payback
            that plays out
            in positioning
            pretending
        to be progress?

will we learn from those
who have wiped out generations,
        that their way is dinosaur
        before the meteor?

will we choose something
besides
    putting another through
                what we paid
                too dearly for?

as the dying animal
clings to past power's purpose,

may we finally learn from
past pain

        to see domination
        as a thing of the past.

BOY PICKED FROM THE COMMONERS

I was prettier when
white men believed
they were
discovering me.

OUT OF THE ASHES

burned all the bridges
that led me away from home.

that chained me
to belonging
to other families.

that could only see me
in the sunlight.

that only allowed in
aspects of me
to remain near
their warmth.

burned all the bridges
'cuz there was no other option.

unseen after
countless christenings.

whatever ratio
breaking my resolve.

taken for granted
the eternal du jour.

learned the hard way
you can't convince a rock
to listen to water.

wish it could've resolved
hallmark easy.

alas, people aren't easy
when refusing to accept
the hurt they bring.

would rather kill you
with denial
than consider their harm.

burned all the bridges
as my get out.

my insecurity still susceptible
to the *but I didn't mean to.*

can still get fooled by a
don't look at it that way.

crippling doubt could rise
off of a
that's not what this is about.

learning to trust myself enough
to break from those
who play people like
house rules monopoly.

molotov'd all of it
to make sure they couldn't
exploit my shame.

burned all the bridges
and don't feel lonely,
away from all I've known.

burned all the bridges
and eager to build
for myself
what I unfairly sought
elsewhere.

burned all the bridges
and they're not supposed
to understand.

burned all the bridges
and realized
many paths must end
to find your own.

burned all the bridges
and can't be claimed
by those
who have
hung me on the wall.

& discovered the power
of honoring self
in order to connect to all.

BEEN WAITING SO LONG TO SEE THIS SHOW

lived long enough to know
I was never crazy,

just trapped
in a vacuum of whiteness.

where unrelenting rightness
turned me into a parrot betraying itself,

surrounded by warped mirrors
in this funhouse nightmare.

almost took my broken
to the corner forever.

almost killed myself literal
while
        puking out
        what kept me
        in well-heated spaces
        filled with artisanal things.

that white people
have it just as hard as everyone else.

that white women
are the most persecuted of all.

that white poets
are actually at a disadvantage.

yet here we are,
in the glorious emergence

of voices affirming
in the 'sphere.

thank god I perused the internet,
or I'd still believe what y'all said
at the beach house
was just in my imagination.

I knew they uplfited one
to better deny oppressing others.

I knew they love other bodies
to project father's sin.

I knew they kept living dolls
to comfort until knights arrive.

I knew they the reason we
invented the term gaslighting.

I knew they would circle the wagons
when spoke out contradicted mask.

I knew they only got enough good deeds
to keep narrative clean in their realm.

I knew they'd forget me
when I no longer martyred for their minor.

    for three eras
    I treated what I lived as a lie.

    got blackout drunk
    on their papier-mâché
    proclamations.

    rejected fellow asians
    only to become unseen
    in front of everyone
    I ate artichokes with.

my beard has greyed
waiting for them to atone.

still sitting in the cost of rejecting
their heritage perceptions.

re-learning how to write
            when my hand not guided by
            desperation to
            pass the test I can't.

though I'm worried
they'll task their next oriental
with absolving their fucked up
            (which I used to do),

can't give passes over coffee
through already closed doors.

can't concern with their fretting
when it's just an excuse
to ignore the borders
surrounding the culture
of their worldview.

so I watch as they attempt to
arc a dirtless enlightenment,

while grateful I've reclaimed
sanity lost in the hot tub.

found confirmation where
their charity can't go.

bit into apples every time
they wanted to put some gloss
on the retreat.

& daily they prove
my prediction:

that one day,
all white people
will lose
their minds.

WORKING ON SAND WILL DROWN YOU

signs of confirmation
often sold by charlatans in suits.

the trap of dichotomy
only serves
those who wish to destroy.

beware the idol
in all its forms framing
the world as war.

as debate club contest
and zero-sum.

the framework of the game
limited in what can be won.

boundless in what could be lost.
basically, all.

the barrage of wrong outcry
begetting right defense,
is the cycle of failure
we build unsustainable cities with.

developing forward requires
more than righteous cause.

leverage is the murder weapon
and you brought cake.

the pressed button in the amygdala
your slow motion kryptonite.
their golden goose.

    the sweet return of rage
    for each drop
    of water on the forehead.

troll upon troll until it leaves
the landscape of lines.

　　　how we play ourselves
believing in how well we play
　　from early inning applause.

know the depth of darkness
or remain in the well alone.

the struggle is not how the writer's room
portrayed it.

this future is not to be won
nor at the designated locations.

you will never be handed
what's required
to escape oppression.

it must be discovered
in the unmapped of their maze.

nurtured when the eye
is turned.

shared in secret
until it can't be taken down
by accounting.

YOU'RE WELCOME

for the words that
expanded your future.

for the ideas that
got you paid
in the writing room.

for the work I did
that made your career
possible.

thank you for coming to my show.

for the insight
that prevented your collapse.

for the healing
you sell knockoffs of
to new followers.

for the concepts
that haunt your life
through their benefit to you.

thank you for presenting
my influence as your awareness.

I used to resent what you got
from what I'd given.

acted like I was owed something
for all you think you've achieved
                with your own two hands.
   plus nothing.

thankfully, graduated from
where you've remained since I bounced.

had to begin honoring
who gave what grew into what gives.

dawning on the endless well within,
              becoming unbothered by
              what you make
              off the seed I planted
              at that lunch meeting.

the consult
that led to your defining project: gratis.

the unveil
that stopped the endless cycle: gratis.

the vouch
that got you taken seriously
in that room:

payment enough that
you will always know it was me.

& while we're here,
you're also welcome
for the gift of

not exploiting your secrets
for advances.

not getting consumed
in elaborate revenge play.

not. calling. you. out. by. name.
in my principle to relegate you
to archetype I warn the world of.

you're welcome to claim
as you need
to feed that avoid.

in the story you tell to
get pity-fucked at parties.

in the story you tell
to sob your way into spotlights.

in the story you tell
to make mutuals pick sides.

this release shall serve
as another step
in my unshackling.

from stalling my life
waiting for your thanks.

from resenting your tidbits,
when destiny awaits.

from the shame of
holding onto the hurt
of loss.

to begin
welcoming in
what
honors me
          as the gift.

EVEN IF
I'M THE
ONLY ONE

I'M A VOICE

for the ways depression can cost you.

for the stunted growth in struggling
to sustain baseline.

for the fear model that
sets the house adrift.

for the body that allows them
to behave like white men.

for those just now discovering
the healthy of boundaries.

for those who've only had blowing it up
to protect from harmful relationships.

for those who hate themselves
into both greatness & collapse.

for that one person curious the cost of
            chasing should the curtain ever close.

for the 40yr old artist
who thought their contribution
                would become their coronation.

for the 40yr old asian
who finally realizes their victimhood
                does not excuse their misogyny.

for the 40yr old asshole
who still disappointing the metaphor
                            of pronouns.

for that kid not satisfied
being less wack than the wackest in their crew.

for asians susceptible
to enabling racism.

for asians fighting history
to not perpetuate supremacy.

for asians who have grown out of
their *dick* size, 'cuz fuck the patriarchy.

> my voice rings out
> for rebels
> too rebellious
> for james dean posters.

for the misunderstood
who keep it moving 'til the world catches up.

for the nuance within the range of the scope
in the context of relation to all.

for those who are willing to say good-bye
to all the rewards that ruin.

for those willing to learn love
'til it becomes the north star of their lives.

for the child I once was,
climbing out of clinging
to other voices
in order to listen to myself
for a change.

WHITE FRIENDS BE LIKE

eager to introduce you
to their new black acquaintance. *see? see?*

are considered courageous
    for eating
        what you grew up being shamed for.

find ways to connect their suburban
to your immigration like it same.

        are all unicorn born of fabergé.
                so this poem isn't about
                any of the friends I've ever had.

if you don't believe me, ask them.

they tell you something they read about tibet,
        waiting to see how your face reacts before
        sharing it at the office party.

they are masters of the grand gesture
as proof of relationship.

love to recount what they've done for you
when it's time to deny all they've done to you.

need 3hrs to solve for absent fathers.
need 3hrs to make sure they're not racist.
need 3hrs to walk through their whole career. again.

ain't got time for your crisis,
they at the crib already and *had a really long day*.

they ask for your undying gratitude
when singing for your supper.

they ask for self-betrayal
when sharing secrets kept from their white cohort.

they ask for the answer
to always end in no responsibility.

my gripe less the myriad
of limitations,
                more the outright
                rejection of their perception
                exposed.

less their ignorance,
        more the willful
        when their 3rd-grade map challenged.

definitely, absolutely
        not about all white people
        (which you have to say about
        all white people,
        when you talk about *any* white people).

just a chink
pondering the sleepover
that began this shit.

my choice to remain regardless
how obvious the playlist
at the barbecue.

the willingness to starve
in order to avoid the louisville slugger
around the corner.

just beginning to name
the unspoken at the ojai wedding.

starting to look back on these friendships
like I do romantic comedies
that trojan horse
under the guise of love.

seeing the parts of the story
writers try to keep hidden.

MERCURY IS ALWAYS IN RETROGRADE

we gotta slow it all down.
        pretending
        to not be overwhelmed
        ain't a good look.

there's too much clapback
in this blame factory.

unable to process the data
before we have to define its purpose.

prone to spreading disinformation
  is a nice way to put this tragedy.

  all these quips
  and still these kids hungry.

  clever to the max
  and still folks living rage.

  the quick dismissal wants
  to clear the slate, but it just
  fills the pit.

no matter how deep you bury it,
what's radioactive will rise.

how can we get ahold of it
when we're still
clutching pearls?

      someone about to argue
      just to feel right in a vacuum.

      this pain keeps coming
      and some asshole just yelling
      faster into the void.

as if rushing one's way
through perpetual grind
turns us into anything
but dust.

these planets are mocking
the incredulous ego of our rationale.

stuck in this unsustainable dreamery.
wishing on stars while
solving for X swept beneath
                the cloud cover.

deception works wonders
when no one takes time to
look under the hood.

CAN'T RUN FAR ENOUGH

it's all happening
& I keep acting like I can escape it.

as if the knife
can stop the hurricane.

as if meditation alone
prevents famine.

as if the race war
is a logical progression
of thought, then poof!

all gone & no loose ends.

as if.
    fat chance.
      no luck roulette
      on this entitlement
          of outcome.

        got coping through addiction
        waiting for saviors to set me free.

        got superhero sequels
        on the brain.

        got off the pedestal
        and saw what muck
        we been festering.

oh, how we cheer for
ourselves to miss the point eloquently.

              dining out
              on luxuries 'til the
              meteor arrives.

wishing on a
revolutionary poster
that can be gift-wrapped
and easy on the conscience.

delving into a silo
to be comforted
while the core quakes.

dimming the lights
so we don't have to
see around corners.

denying the measles metaphor
in every blinding privilege.

& I'm sitting in my
complaints box
begging to be read
by the powers that be
(as if I could spark more
than a head nod).

we be powerless
in our concession to masters
that knew we'd never read
the terms of service.

& I'm doing just enough
to be ahead of wack place,

like that will keep the wolf
from bearing down
on my neck.

as if I can make the solution
what's agreeable to the stomach.

the gut receives
what the tongue is tricked by.

want to share the next movement,
        but only know
        what's wrong with the rote choreo
        we think will win the championship.

it's still escapism
if you can't
        let in the world as it is
        to understand who you are.

most wake choosing
to walk backwards to stay
along familiar lines.

and all of these go bags
spell out where the living
are unwilling to work.

ain't no costa rica for any of us
to go to.

can't think your way out of
the dragon's lair, especially
when the smell of fear
draws the fire
of your reckoning.

WHAT TO LOOK FOR

the last thing you wanna do
is believe it's everyone in a red hat.

pied pipers play discernment
through details
           leading you down
           dire agendas.

truth in a bubble
is always waiting to pop on you.

look for what is revealed
in the unsaid.

listen for the tell
beneath the gesture.

the predator feigns disinterest in his stalk.
the curator has language proving he not racism.
the executive sits in a room of his design.

indignant response is a ruse of the powerful
to send us spiraling into madness.

alpha absoluting is the doubt gun
eager to watch you bleed out.

their trick
is to keep your eyes
        conditioned on bolds,
    while they take
    the bank
    out your hands.

they love bias
leaving concerns on the table.

will lead the witness so you
don't wonder why it doesn't feel as progress
as you're sold.

use how we gauge experience
        through the lens of others' essays
                to content us living lines.

can we extract
        the *what a white man says it is*
        from the equation?

can we go sans colony
        to choose beyond the dynamic
                of bondage?

can we feel a scope
        instead of quiz each other
        on right answers?

knowing what to look for
prevents the dictation luring us
away from the truth.

what can you see in me
        when no longer
        trying to place
        where I belong
        in the city of checked boxes?

GROWING UP BANANA

how I learned what they say
when no black people are around.

what made ordering at sizzler
less gawk fest for family.

which gave me access
contrary to the world of 80s sitcom.

that I used like a tourist
who thinks they can move somewhere
after a nice weekend.

getting clowned for your eyes
at the sleepover
feels like being seen to the invisible.

which is better than
being esl ridiculed daily.

which is better than
being blamed for the auto industry.

which is better than
being a walking enemy of war.

which is the lie I kept scribbling
in my journal,

        unaware I was writing
        a postdated letter to my younger self
        on how to discern
                between survival & fulfillment.

KEEP IT MOVING

from our mouths spring
empire without consent.

move the limbs to remind
where communication was born.

before the word
named what it do,
the body
revealed who we are
to each other.

how have I been
defined as foreign
before I was born?

don't let them know you're a chink.
don't let them mistake it for kung fu.
don't let them put stereotype to it.

sequence of the movement
evolves us out of fixed sentences.

signals in the motion
transcend construct of faces.

symbols born of moves
rising beyond where words
can go.

who have I tried to be
to touch connection denied?

show them you can find the one.
show them you are in rhythm.
show them you got music in you.

mama made me a dancer
for all the songs lost across
the ocean.

the music she longs to become
            what she's never heard anyone say.

tinikling 'til filipinos know where we from.
b-boy in the bronx 'til puerto ricans affectionately me
chino.
rave in okc 'til the warehouse desegregates the body.
rap city at every school dance 'til all they see is hip-hop.
tap, jazz, and ballet 'til white girl learns my name.

who am I
when we are no longer
accounting for translation?

let me belong in this house party.
let me belong in this wedding.
let me belong in this barrio fiesta.
let me belong in this battle.
let me belong
            in this skin
            pleading past poses
            to be more than seen.

this is the dance
of a boy raised in a silenced era.

in the back of the electric slide,
finding the flow.

in the soul train line
to show off for a chance.

in the circle getting free
in four four time.

'til the movement
mines the breaks
breaking all from
the cypher's confines.

now,
       may I have this dance?

THEY KNOW NOT WHAT THEY DO 2: THE RETURN

we live in a world
dying by the literal.

divided assuming
intention.

caught up in
truth marketing.

unaware of definition
coding.

consumed by
reactionomics.

overwhelmed by
absolute claim.

sans processing
past first impression.

obsessed with
the obvious silo.

a trillion ways to debate club.
a trillion details forced meaning.
a trillion chyrons framing truth.
a trillion unchecked presentations.
a trillion wins leading nowhere.

stuck in the stating,
no rewards for exploring,
too many keep cycling through
early childhood games.

wanting it to be answer,
terrified to further question,

surrounded by
snake oil failing
the festering wound.

this is our lot in life
when we swept up
in the lie
that we can make this
a movie.

can't edit the necessary
on behalf
of the spectacular
and expect to learn
how to climb out of the well.

this is what happens
when the buildup
calcifies the hand
into a fixed position.

clutching at air
as if it holy grail.

always holding on
when the handle is burning.

only letting in
the metaphors
that make
sugar hills
out of
greek tragedy.

no honest choices
making the truth
a trophy
for conquerors.

LOOKING BACK ON WHAT ONCE

been weighing the value of
what was written while I wanted
white approval so desperately.

what the words mean now aware
of the insecurity driving my expression.

what I didn't see caught up in the glory
as solution for all I refused to face.

not to wrong my way, but to account
for what I ignored in assumption.

how the brilliant line
disguises the act out
of the unseen given platform.

how the truth got muddled
by incel ideas unchecked in supremacy spaces.

how the story only revealing enough aspects
to hide all the harm along for the ride.

the cost of genius
when what inspires the chinese boy in minnesota
may harm the chinese girl in new york.

when writing the real feeling
creatively hides its destructive potential.

when what strangers adored in past work
becomes folks' present pain.

and the list goes on,
trying to dump all this bath water
without self-hatin' myself
into throwing out the baby.

none of us
can ace the purity test.

all of us are living arcs
that can't dodge history
no matter what textbooks imply.

each of us are tasked to shed
what shaped the monster in us
                              for the master.

and here I am,
putting a drop in the bucket.

at the step of
acknowledgement rising
into the thorough.

so far from the whole,
but keep exorcising illusions written well.

for it's taken me so long to recognize
that supremacy
is capable
of applauding different
so long as
it's delivering same.

WHITE GIRLFRIEND NO. 3

you're gonna have to
leave
way more
than your shoes
at the door
when you enter
my mama's house.

BILLIONAIRE ON BILLIONAIRE VIOLENCE

because others
are always the first,
we assume
that they the never.

everyone needs a refresher course
on the cue.

on the endgame
of greed checkers.

on the pact
that gets broken
in the finale.

every comfort believes
its softness eternal.

we get used to being untouched
by current circumstance.

the mountaintop
is invincible to those
of limited perspective.

the rival you sleep with
becomes the friend who
fucks you
when everyone else
has been kicked out
of the party.

sent to the camps.
razed with the village.
vanished from
the demographics.

first they came for
is not just a tale for the worker.

the power of men
is unquenchable thirst.

there is only one mouth
that can drink it all.

and asset accumulation
won't save these boyz
chasing highlander.

who see no need in peons
while the knife sharpens in
their neighbor's house.

who never fear
those struggling to survive the holidays
from their skyscraper construct.

a sweet liquor warming
smug lips by the fireside.

as if the ruled will always be.
as if partners will not turn envy.
as if kingdom will never fall.

woe be the conqueror
who runs out of the conquered.

with no one left
to send into darkness.
shivering by the embers,
alone in the echo chamber.

reminiscing on who
he could've helped

before realizing
ten billion merely words
when only ten remain.

WALLOW 9000

they give me pity fucks
for who I used to be.

all that's faded
is rolled into my coping.

the binge watch
is my favorite deadly sin.

cost of internalizing blame:
everything you are.

I'm wading through
on faith,
              but flailing it.

try to put on a smiling face,
but can't lose the pretender eyes.

soft sorrow around
the edges, screaming.

get out to myself
so stifled
I can only mime it
behind 4th walls.

which has no
thinkpiece for it.

the melancholy
of this melodrama so severe,

I don't know
what's good anymore.

DON'T BE THAT GUY

who always has a reason
for not being racist.

who gets so incensed by the call out,
he suddenly lists
every non-racist thing
he's ever done.

who behaves as if
get over it
is something
all y'all papa johns would do.

who thinks racism
is what tenured institutions
dissertate it is.

who only sees racism
as burning cross.

who believes his lot in life
means he could never be.

who has donations, posts,
friends, and rallies on hand
as a shield from accountability.

who can't see the nuance of it
through tailored threads.

who is so afraid of blame,
he refuses to consider responsibility.

who shows up on halloween,
shamelessly in blackface,
yelling out
to the whole room,

"what's your fucking problem?"

YOU CAN ALWAYS CHANGE YOUR MIND

check in on your trust,
before someone runs away with it.

predators softening us up
for the kill.

ranchers putting cattle
in a system of calm
to beguile them to slaughter.

    the phrase
    coded to your beliefs.

    the body representing
    frames designated safe.

    the stated narrative
    used to reflect your story.

who taught us trust
without considering
the diabolical of seeming?

'cuz there is someone
always presenting well enough
to fool you.
        use you.
                take it all
                and portray it
                as freely given.

'til ya trust them enough
to carry out their agenda
        in exchange for
        your extinction.

know the words that engender blindness
                                        to the asking's
                                        inherent
                                        betrayal of self.

        mentor asks you
        to commit fraud
        for their son's spoiled.

        old friend tells you
        to be racist
        so she can keep her spot.

        partner suggests you
        stop working with everyone else
        'cuz they not whiteboard.

        org wants you to
        fundraise in the name of children
        the money will never reach.

        candidate demands
        undying support,
        even as they veer
        from why you chose them
                                        and towards
                                        what will end you.

        vigilance to look for
        daggers in the dark.

        disease
        in the distracting smile.

        rot spreading
        in the cracks uncounted
        at appraisal.

may your trust
be a living document

and not a fixed
set of terms.

may your trust
be treated more precious
than the petty
it has been abused for.

may you remember this
before the next time, beau.

for the greatest gifts inspire
the most adept thieves.

you will be lost forever
if you ever let them have
power-of-attorney
over your treasures.

MY BEEF ISN'T WITH YOU

thought I'd humiliate you in a poem
as a lesson taught.

but I've vowed not to do my version of

securing lies
with mutuals
    to secure a chair.

we all know that's your thing.

                        to not go
                where you've gone
                in your resistance
            to reconcile childhood

        is the pillar of healing
        I never saw coming

        as I work through my rage
        over your misdeeds
        viewed as justified.

every minute of breath blaming your jerkitude
weakens relationship with power within.

sharing your wackness as absolute
just adds to the broken in this world.

causes me to avoid the responsibility
I'm tired of placing elsewhere.

besides, you are not
the heart of the ocean.

just an archetype of costume jewelry,
found in every town square.

rather than rail on
the counterfeit
of your particular display,

better to show others
how to spot
              any fugazi.

for there is nothing gained
in making you the one,

when you're just a local rep
we gotta teach these children
stranger danger for.

ADVICE TO YOUNG ASIANS GROWING UP IN AMERICA

if you don't want to die inside,
do not hang out with only white people.*

it will serve the world you want to live in more
if you uplift black women instead of chase white approval.*

the american dream as we've been taught
won't provide all you'll need in this country.*

you can say chink, but in many contexts,
it's gonna get lost in translation.*

most of y'all gotta get more inclusive than
which types of chinks support your quest to chart.*

taking it out on foreign nationals
don't make you more american to anyone on campus.*

if you do not honor the generations before you,
you will be forgotten by the generations after you.*

you do not have to trust someone just because
the movies have indoctrinated you to trust them.*

believe your asian friends
before waiting for a white man's writings to confirm it.*

do not bring the wars of our homelands here.*

you will never be black or white,
so no need to play into it.*

dick size leads to madness,
which is why you need to
work on your misogyny now.*

and if you ever doubted, racism, too.*

which is why you must
stay ever vigilant that you do not become
a stan for supremacy.*

never listen to another asian person
simply because they are one.*

stop eating so much fucking pizza.*

*in my experience.

POETRY FOR THE PEOPLE

before the unicorn
becomes the spokesperson.

before all are honored
the same way
only white men once were.

before the poets
form a country club.

before the reading turns
into rage revival.

before the word
loses itself in words.

before verse
synonymous with propaganda.

before it all sours literal.

before metaphor solely
an escape route.

before we sacrifice humanity
for definition.

before everyone entitled
to pass judgment.

before stories silenced
by pedestal riots.

before self lost forever
writing for praise.

before the body
is taken from us again.

before you throw away
that folded love in cursive.

before you give up
on stating your raw
for future's sake.

before you stop
letting the seep
of beauty
transform your
relationship
with the wind.

before
dictators make game
of way.

before cause
shuts the mouth.

before possibility
is only in poems.

NOTHING FOR GRANTED

ALL FOR LOVE

EVERY ASIAN ASPIRING NEEDS TO HIRE
BEAU SIA, BASICALLY

all my lovelies on the come up,
the game still ain't the same for you.

the ceiling less a great wall
visible from space,

>   more all-consuming fog
>   unseen in the shadow of power.

unwritten rules abound
in places yet acknowledged
by cartographers.

path still ends before the finish line.

>   even as progress propagandas
>   that it's all gravy.

the way paved to evolve your place
doesn't change the fact that
you still have one.

>   to those toasting
>   the bankroll of
>   their entitlement.

>   to those getting work
>   off your trauma's grace.

>   to those demanding you
>   keep striving
>   as a reaction to them.

I paid the price to discover
what lies beyond
the story of glory

told possible
for us.

all the boobytraps
data didn't tell you about.

every friendly gesture
        hiding a deadly blade.

        the slowsand of
        lingering vampires.

        each archetype
        that will
        exploit your trust for clout.

codes within conditioned definitions
keeping you comforted by
                false supporters.

        how you may be uplifted
        to crash harder.

    the big fall
    the moment
    you quit living for
    the love of milk.

I lost my mind
        so you don't have to.

I wore all the masks to
find out what's behind the cellar door.

I spent these years
wandering the wasteland of washed.

I know how to keep your rise
from being
at the mercy

of monuments
to eras
that erased you.

& it can all be yours
for the introductory low cost
of

releasing
the ache
to be embraced
by ghosts.

removing
the blindfold
to supremacy.

reclaiming
the house
you've kept secret
in order to move.

when you're ready
to pay the price,

call me.

PROTECT BLACK WOMEN

If you want to save yourself.

If you believe
in the future.

If you get that
it can't be done alone.

If you think you're
not a racist.

If you woke up today wondering
how can I make the world a better place?

If you retweeted 9 black women
and still see dead people.

If you visited somewhere colonized
and bought a souvenir.

If you got
amazon prime.

If you have children.

If you ever laughed
while watching.

protect black women with
what you choose in the presence of other people.

when you hear the way
they aren't believed for being.

when you walk down the street
knowing you're not the target.

when they aren't allowed
in the halls of power.

what you do to uplift one
will impact us all.

their magic
is the potion that will save us.

how we protect black women
is reflection of how
we honor our humanity.

protect black women
to cut the cord of patriarchy.

prove you're more than the slogan
used to confirm an idea.

show you're willing to nurture
what threatens ownership.

repeat the mantra
until this dimming
reverses course.

protect black women
and all else will follow.

ALL YOUR TALENT IS INFLATED BY BEING YOU KNOW WHAT

apparently we're in a meritocracy.
I guess if all we're doing is vacuuming, sure.

it's astounding the assumptions
at one's disposal
when gifted with supremacy skin.

the value of confidently stating
afforded certain dicks.

having a riff turn into a direction
in a room full of others eager to
get past the foyer.

getting paid on the scale of potential,
not the hours you toil
for another's title.

failures less condemnation
more learning process.

when your tornado
is treated like a breeze.

when ineptitude opens a door
to collaboration.

when the cost of your words
aren't counted
on the scale of demerits.

everyone knows
english in practice
is a master of disguise.

we are all created equal a phrase
        that permits imposing neglect.

   bootstrap idioms
   marking failure what
   clearly circumstance.

when the tale treated as reality
is in defiance of truth,

beware the body
that benefits from delusion.

beware the price
of being near those
who exhaust themselves
maintaining lies
to eat off racism.

beware the way
you'll doubt the undeniable
reading about the might
of crybabies
obsessed with fables.

do not take the bait,
for their score is handicapped
by ancestors' hate.

"GREATEST HUMAN ARTIST OF ALL TIME"

we say the craziest
for a semblance of agency.

we get caught in another's game
trying to prove our unique.

we eat the soup
and never question the taste of hemlock.

we lash out so creatively
when we're not heard
for who we are.

we tell ourselves lies
to salve the pain
of environments that
deny existence.

we upset at what we're not given,
and instead of
            considering how it
            not meant for us,

            try to take boldly
            what we can't grasp.

fed *toooo* long
on suspension-of-disbelief,

we start believing our be anything
possible through simple exertion of will.

we are chasing dreams edited for length.
we are wearing see-through masks.
we are handing out titles
like all credentials verified to santa.

capable of so much,
yet limit ourselves
in the bestness of
what they give awards for.

of course we gotta be better
than anyone's ever
        just to be worthy of remnants.

you don't need the almanacs
to witness it
    throughout western civ.

we been killing each other
to call ourselves the greatest.

a comedic idea
to those
allowed to be human

without concern that
being mediocre
will get them erased.

THIS ONE GOES OUT TO THE FUTURE

in which it will be impossible
to get
what is now immediate.

in which everyone discovers
they're next in line.

for disenfranchisement.
for de-activation.
for dying horribly in an
unimaginable way.

it doesn't have to be this way,
but clearly knowing the secret isn't enough.

wonder how time will betray
this desire to control outcome.

look at us wishing on a world
that remains unmoved by
all the right words.

what we've learned
could make a utopia
                hasn't changed the way

        we punch each other
        for not
        enabling the worst in us.

we resigned attitude
towards the collateral
of this chaos
we perpetuate in the name of.

we think
          as if the planet wants to know first
                    how you wanna extinct?

keep living in everyone's favorite
einstein quote.

painting the house a different color
isn't storm prevention.

when the planet comes for us,
it will be because
of what we did to each other

when we thought we weren't.

when we were
fussing with the perfection
of seeming.

when we decided
that it's better to look the part
than earn the way.

IF I WAS BORN WHITE

I would smell worse.

my skin would be less soft.

you'd be able
to tell my age.

it's just science.

if I still had brown eyes,
they'd no longer be foreign.

if I still had black hair,
        it would be intriguing.

if I still stood 5'8"
        I'd still be short in america.

        the culture here
        quantifies along
        frontier bias.

                but I digress.

the fluency would be
assumed.

the belonging would be
given at the roller rink.

the hostess would notice
I'm standing here waiting
for a table.

my appearance
ain't only the hardship of
the invisible pawn.

being white wouldn't just be
warnings
instead of tickets.

I'd be lost to my ancestry
and frankenstein it a shield.

I'd miss out on other cultures
fixated on their food.

I'd be way less talented
and believe
every praise not conditioned.

which still wouldn't bother
my bank account
             & probably
                not me, either.

would have a shot at
being loved
       even if the skill level
       was basic to the aliens.

being important
even if the resume
left much to be desired.

oh, to be seen
through the lens of potential,
even on worst hair days.

as a janitor,
there would
probably be a nobility
attached to my choice.

the teachers would
elevate my service in speeches.

how my work viewed as poetry
the way I
merely sweep the floor.

WHERE THE WIND COMES SWEEPING DOWN THE PLAIN

I told y'all I'd make it one day,
but never stopped to thank you for it.

    they pay me for the pain I felt
    from the casual way you demeaned.

    they give me opportunities
    from what I sculpted your rejections into.

    they praise the meager courage
    of refusing to be the joke in public.

jokes on us,
'cuz what has the work done
as this unleashing of hate
brushfires across continents?

how have I healed the past
if today reminds me of the 90s?

        don't buy that jap crap t-shirts
        on students & teachers.
        .

        neo-nazis strolling the halls
        with pride.

        the cacophony of joy when
        bombings kill brown people.

feels like oklahoma won't let me run
from what it was trying to show us.

surrounded in the suburbs
and still we never questioned
what we were feeding
in our do nothing.

yet, in the thick humidity of bigotry,
you still came over to bogart castlevania.

we found common bond in goth sirens
calling out how alone we felt as teens.

you didn't let john fuck me up at that rave
for my yellow reminder
in his heil house music.

started gathering these moments
to one day full picture the plains
instead of crafting vanity narratives.

doesn't change the egg roll you adored
in private, but never stood up for in history.

won't soften the slur you sounded
when at your most outlandish.

isn't enough to pretend
knowing my place at every turn didn't happen.

the past contains more truth
than what fits on a side,

how the foreshadowing of race war fantasy
also inkling of possibility that
maybe I put a chink in your armor.

had enough sleepovers that
you're not harassing immigrants
when you're short on rent.

did enough extra credit
that thai jerry isn't seen as a threat.

lived enough moments
that incline you to welcome strangers

who'd be seen as foreign
had we not b-boyed together.

maybe learn to apply what only retrospect
would teach us how to heal.

to honor past friendships
more than caveat emptor lessons
and rose-tinted memory.

give that time a chance
to be more than looking back
on what could've been
had we known.

MISOGYNY IS A CULT WE'RE BORN INTO

that's it.
that's the tweet.

BEFORE IT GETS PASSED DOWN PERMANENTLY

let's wake up
not overwhelmed by the unpredictable.

let those who harm us
stop being those who haunt us.

blame the world less
and work the world as we know it.

we don't have to take personally
what's absent in the lies others compass by.

don't have to make it
everything or nothing
for ease of placement.

our parents arrived here to give us more
than knowledge recognized by the canon.

their sacrifice was for more
than the papers we been collecting.

our success will be more than
what we buy that they couldn't.

there's an opportunity in our family
to not live the lash out and
        the dramatic good-bye.

the gifts they gave us can provide
more than american dreams
        that deny unalienable
        in the penthouse.

even as we get genius on pyramid
of needs,
        we can develop sphere of
        honoring emotions.

how dare we not recognize
our capacity.

all we are doesn't have to be
what has always been.

there's a turning point
in each generation.

we can evolve how we do the same
to each other, or we can evolve.

for we do not have to become our parents
if we can will ourselves to understand them
more than define them.

       lead this relationship
       to more than making them into an ideal
       or a villain.

we can spend the rest of this unguaranteed time
rejecting what we don't like 'til we become the 2.0

or we can develop thorough
until we grow out of
what kept them from becoming
what their sacrifice
has gifted us with
in order
to beyonder
the line of legacy.

OCCAM'S RAZOR

been trying to think how to write
like all the people of color that
white people are fawning over.

been wanting to write like the
youngs who are taking over the
social media I not understand still.

been hoping to compose poems
like the generations after me who
got asian written better than I lived.

been fearing I'll write like the age
of misogyny that raised my view
and gave me the juice to eat off art.

been worried the writing will be
the obvious victimhood of entitled
east asians complaining oblivious.

been procrastinating so in my mind
all the words can have the impact I
want them to without ever having to.

been re-working the work as if I can
use words to transform relationship
with myself in ways words can't. ugh.

been dying to be as courageous as
poets of now as if I never was a one
and how did I lose myself in this?

been praying the words will not only
arrive authentic but beloved by all
the people I'm afraid think I'm wack.

been angrily struggling through words
like gotta prove something about my
writing more than what I need to share.

been living in a loop of how to write
in a way that doesn't lose without
considering how it could lose me.

been over-thinking my words because
of the trauma of envy circles that has
led to what my life's like in the shadow.

been dreaming I will reclaim it all but
have yet to take my moment as I
struggle through the permissions of.

FUCK MY DOUBT X FINDING MY WAY

NOTE TO SELF WORK

get there before sundown.

feed yourself
only with what nurtures.

let the process of shedding
be joyous in its eternity.

create and call it creation.

tell lashing out that
it isn't worthy of your song.

beat the drum
instead of yourself.

beat the drum when hands
want to become fists.

beat the drum to get
beneath the surface.

jump off the bed.
welcome waves in the tub.
cook as if dancing.

be a metaphor
when literal is too much.

cry into your journal
as if it is rising's way.

praise into your journal
like you ain't apologizing
to no one for shine.

claim into your journal,
for there's no need
to die waiting.

be too vibrant for lingering
on those who neglect.

too awww
to keep treating yourself
so poorly.

be more than knowing.

in case you need encouragement,
I'mma share
that memory
you tucked away,

scared you'd be laughed at
trying for more than
drowning spectacularly.

that shows you beyond
the bad beats.

who you were before
that season you've forgotten.

to remind
that every victory counts
and that you're
one step closer today.

THE CULT

is never witnessed
at the surface of it.

you will be misled
looking for amulets.

the incantation of gibberish
    not necessarily a sign.

how will you know
what to look for, unaware
you wander lost
in what you long for?

        hunger to belong
        is why the uniform
        gets put on.

the shame of our hurt
    becomes the weapon they give us
    to use against ourselves.

consequences of neglect
stretch long after the era of.

    what would wake you
    from the communal clap
    to recognize the indoctrination?

    what would wake you
    from a smile's spell in order
    to sense insidious will?

    what would wake you
    from the pomposity of purpose

to feel the punishing preening
of the leader's ego?

for we are in a world so lacking,
we'll eat any candy that kills us
                just to feel sweet.

        we doubt ourselves into
        looping first impressions
        to stay in devolving states.

                we get bound by
                our unchecked grief co-opted
                by familiar archetypes.

we end up caught in the tornado,
                waiting for the cobra
                to show itself,

when leaving
is the only way to test
whether or not
it's hidden in the basket
                where you've placed your prayer.

path takes you elsewhere?
become the one who abandoned the children.

call out the great leader?
those addicted to belonging will reject you.

get all the way the fuck away?
you will be erased from the story book.

cast out as if you never were,
while acolytes scrub your memory
from the shelves of its history.

it's the hot new hollywood.
it's family running from plantations.
it's club only one color exists.
it's your little circle of asshole friends.
it's a community space
around the corner from where you work.

cult not by the what of it,
    rather grown from the
    resentful entitlement
    of gurus.

look for the tell in the bond
that hides bondage.

how it ignores your pain
to make you feel reborn in its arms.

how it voices the promise
you've always longed to hear.

how it is immediate
in its lovefest.

rushing you to the altar
before you can question the vow.

asking you to sacrifice everything
for a taste of shine.

masquerading as the answer
while taking no questions
that challenge what you've been
asked to do in the name of.

WOULD YOU LIKE TO PLAY A GAME OF WAR?

your enemy has
    the weather dominator
    & you trying
    to shoot at clouds.

strategy is more than
what the opposing team
releases publicly.

this seems like a given,
                but not
                by the way we act.

we see war as a narrative
of stickers that glow in the dark.

      written history fixated
      on the parts
      that serve our future defeat.

      detailery camouflages
      the battles we're losing
      each time we feel
      like we've won a point.
                made our case.
   told someone off
    & got their goat
        etc etc.

or maybe we still don't see this war,
because we have hulu without commercials.

because we already booked
tickets to burning man.

because we got funner things to do
than read what section of
the art of war this is from.

what instruments are we using
that misdiagnose these signs?

how is there no doppler
for the slight between friends
that ends communities?

why are we looking for catapults
in the middle of crowded shelters?

I wake up every day
and watch masses
        fight over bedazzled scraps
        while the source
        drains into
        the mouths of monsters.

I watch the screen
and folks can't be bothered outside
the realm of petty resentments.

I walk the world and too few
        hear the weapon coming.

gestating through civilizations,
                hidden within distractions,
en route
to all the places
we've failed to protect
from unintended consequences.

all the choices we thought
were just having a laugh.

every strike we've felt entitled to
in our bathtubs of pain.

a reckoning on the cusp
of irreversible.

the signal to acknowledge
the weight of scale before
the sale becomes final.

FOR ALL MY WHITE FRIENDS ACTUAL

didn't kill myself because you kept reaching out,
even if I didn't respond to text.

means much you do this
when I am wallow over the choices
                  I keep punishing myself for.

thank you for walking with me
in places you never thought dangerous.

campus in western pennsylvania.
amusement park in oklahoma.
wendy's off I-40 in arizona.

thank you for walking me into
places you never saw velvet ropes.

the luxurious hors d'ouvres festival.
the conference of neckties.
the stage where poetry is milk only.

thank you for walking to me
when I couldn't get out of bed.

midtown box that swallowed me.
venice flat filled with lopsided mirrors.
canyon castle where I cast contemplation
into the abyss.

your visits most felt when all I had to give
                was a pocket full of excuses.

thank you for listening to all
            the things I said about white people,
     without needing me to qualify you
     as exception to the rule.

for not going defensive over
	what would cost you to consider.

for compassion
when I burned out on holding up white crisis
and needed cave years.

for the faith that I'd find my way back
to what I gave up for sparklers.

thank you for giving me more than
one chance to be in your life.

thank you for not asking me to carry
racism you may have for someone else.

thank you for trying to see
how I navigate different
regardless how I'm spoken of.

thank you for giving
when it wasn't a convenient way
to later proclaim yourself my savior.

thank you for the way you used your power
in our relationship.

defending me to your elk city friends
who never saw me outside the vietnam war.

explaining me to jersey friends
who only chased me when they were younger.

uplifting me to friends who only let
folks like me do their laundry.

thank you
for not manipulating me into
	a role that enables ignorance.
	a role that plays boyfriend placeholder.

a role that makes me
            carry the boulder of lies
        amongst white pages.

thank you for sparing me from that.

for never calling my
outfits weird,
            for never exclaiming me crazy,

        for never treating me as too serious
        when the joke played on the piano
is that I'm the joke.

you've shown me the failings
of other white people
    who've danced through my days.

you've helped me break from
                    all the white people
                    who wanted me
                            to stay
                in the french of my name.

you've given me a gift
that prevents any's wackness
from turning into my hate.

I can't thank the 5 of you enough

for all you've revealed about the other 63.

CHINK IN YOUR ARMOR

be like water
with a code switch
so cold
it's absolute.

for the culture
even when
expression
doesn't compute.

rhymed it for the back
and keep testing
the resolute.

me got nothing to lose,
so who else wanna fuck with
hollywood beau?

I'll leave the whole party
even if it's
     the last one ever.

I'll go undercover to
    hero's journey the help.

I'll break a community
to show it never really was a one.

they don't got words for what
       I've worn to your event.

how I can fuck up your whole
       history of perception
    from what I keep in my closet.

I'll cosmic fool until
your lineage

no longer
passed down in false volumes.

henry IV all over the public square,
          'til these falstaffs awaken
            as the cronies they are.

            throw up a jumanji set
            just to hear the sound it makes
            in the hater house.

you woke the dragon and now
you decryin' these melted towers?

        I'll make metaphor
        of all you touch.

        I'll win the lottery
        to save beat street.

        I'll irreverent my way
        into every heart
        and kick out all our exes.

        yeah, I'm that chink.

        I'll turn the ocean
                into your island.
the prize
into your shackle.
                        the beloved circle
                        into the space
        where spells go to die.

pages can't contain me.
& sages can't comprehend.

stages are wherever I be.
& ages converge where I'm sent.

I predicted the thing
you never saw coming.

I let verse go borderless
before it became my cage.

I foreshadow 50yr plans
                while they still
                lapping up
                all the caviar moments.

what you call me
becomes your minotaur's lair.

easy to kill
and already forever
against your will.

jokes on you, sucker.

you've mistaken this game
as your own.

my play
a prophecy
unfolding the boy
rising en route
to home

au Sia is a Tony Award-winning poet, featured on all seasons of
O's *Def Poetry*, and is the author of *The Undisputed Greatest Writer
All Time*. Through his poetry, he explores the possibility of metaphor
ond the poem. Through his poems, he expresses the potential of
taphor to develop out of hurt, rise from being bound to role, and to
ch purpose more potent than power.

For catalog information:
notacult.media

Not a Cult's Spring + Fall 2020 catalog

hours inside out by Isabella Preisz
ISBN: 978-1-945649-38-7

Well Played by Beau Sia
ISBN: 978-1-945649-39-4

Zigzags by Kamala Puligandla
ISBN: 978-1-945649-34-9

Birthday Girl by Sheila Sadr
ISBN: 978-1-945649-40-0